Moonlight ☽ Editions

Mark Twain
Poor little
Stephen
Girard

illustrated by Nicollet

Schocken Books · New York

The man lives in Phila-
delphia, who, when young
and poor, entered a bank,
and says he: "Please sir,
don't you want a boy?"
And the stately personage
said: "No, little boy, I
don't want a little boy."

The little boy, whose heart was too full for utterance, chewing a piece of licorice stick he had bought with a cent stolen from his good and pious aunt, with sobs plainly audible, and with great globules of water running down his cheeks, glided silently down the marble steps of the bank. Bending his noble form, the bank man dodged behind a door, for he thought the little boy was going to shy a stone at him.

But the little boy picked up something, and stuck it in his poor but ragged jacket.

"Come here, little boy," and the little boy did come here; and the bank man said: "Lo, what pickest thou up?" And he answered and replied: "A pin."

And the bank man said: "Little boy, are you good?" and he said he was. And the bank man said: "How do you vote? – excuse me, do you go to Sunday school?" and he said he did.

Then the bank man took down a pen made of pure gold, and flowing with pure ink, and he wrote, on a piece of paper: *"St. Peter,"* and he asked the little boy what it stood for, and he said: *"Salt Peter."* Then the bank man said it meant *"Saint Peter."*

Then the little boy said: "Oh!"
Then the bank man took the little boy into partner-ship, and gave him half the profits and all the capital.

And he married the bank man's daughter, and now all he has is all his, and all his own, too.

2

My uncle told me this story, and I spent six weeks in picking up pins in front of a bank. I expected the bank man would call me in and say: "Little boy, are you good?" and I was going to say "Yes"; and when he asked me what *"St. John"* stood for, I was going to say *"Salt John."*

But the bank man wasn't anxious to have a partner, and I guess the daughter was a son, for one day says he to me; "Little boy, what's that you're picking up?" Says I, awfully meekly, "Pins." Says he: "Let's see 'em." And he took 'em, and I took off my cap all ready to go in the bank and become a partner, and marry his daughter.

But I didn't get an invitation. He said: "Those pins belong to the bank, and if I catch you hanging around here any more I'll set the dog on you!" Then I left, and the mean old cuss kept the pins. Such is life as I find it.